Cuba's Evolution

P133685
P063789
FORD

Classic cars lined up in the Parque Central, Havana, opposite the Capitolio.

Cuba's Evolution

Columbus to Castro

Kim Buddee

Schiffer Publishing Ltd
4880 Lower Valley Road • Atglen, PA 19310

For Frances

Library of Congress Control Number: 2017935511

Cover design by John Cheek
Type set in Cubana, Playfair & Open Sans

ISBN: 978-0-7643-5312-3
Printed in China

Published by Schiffer Publishing, Ltd.
4880 Lower Valley Road
Atglen, PA 19310
Phone: (610) 593-1777; Fax: (610) 593-2002
E-mail: Info@schifferbooks.com
Web: www.schifferbooks.com

For our complete selection of fine books on this and related subjects, please visit our website at www.schifferbooks.com. You may also write for a free catalog.

Schiffer Publishing's titles are available at special discounts for bulk purchases for sales promotions or premiums. Special editions, including personalized covers, corporate imprints, and excerpts, can be created in large quantities for special needs. For more information, contact the publisher.

We are always looking for people to write books on new and related subjects. If you have an idea for a book, please contact us at proposals@schifferbooks.com.

CONTENTS

PREFACE

People travel for business, family, education, holidays, beaches and sun, and mountains and snow. Some take a trip to escape, to be somewhere different, to experience foreign lands and languages, or to explore exotic places with the possible chance of adventure. In many cases they are also time traveling.

A man dwelling in an outback cattle station in central Australia is transported to the future when he encounters Tokyo, with its high tech bullet trains and futuristic buildings. A woman from the modern suburbs of Dallas, Texas, is taken back thousands of years while exploring temples and artifacts among the ancient ruins of Egypt. In the twenty-first century, such dramatic contrasts are becoming harder to find. Globalization is creating a dreary sameness around the planet. We encounter identical banks, fast food chains, simultaneously streamed television shows, multi-national clothing brands, and sports teams. Here and there are pockets in the world largely untouched. Once such places were cut off and lost in time because of their geographical remoteness, but today it is more than likely due to political factors.

When I visited Burma (now Myanmar) in early 2012, the country was on the verge of opening up politically and economically after over fifty years of isolation from the outside world. Clapped out rusted cars bumped along broken empty streets. People were transported in ancient, slow trains and old buses converted from World War II trucks. ATMs and credit cards were rare, there were confusing dual currencies, and electricity was so unreliable that the streets were cluttered with stinking diesel generators. The Burmese still dressed in their national costume, the skirt-like *longhi*, and the women wore traditional white paste on their faces called *thanaka*. Buildings, totally unchanged from their former long gone heydays, were crumbling or neglected, yet were still occupied by their poor, long suffering tenants. My record of the former capital city Rangoon (Yangon) became my book *ONCE WAS BURMA*.

It was evident that a number of the same funky, frozen-in-time characteristics of the former pariah state Burma could be found in Cuba. It had also closed its doors to the free world in the early 1960s, and adopted an authoritarian centralist socialist form of

Farmers in Pinar del Rio Province make their early morning journey to work by horse and cart.

> “I have come here to bury the last remnant of the Cold War in the Americas.”
>
> –President Barack Obama

government. There were other parallels between these countries, like the old cars, run-down buildings, and dual currencies. But unlike Burma, in Cuba there was no Nobel Peace Prize winning dissident imprisoned for more than twenty years, adored by the public and waiting to save the country. What would trigger changes in Cuba?

Suddenly, in December 2014, US President Obama began a process of re-engagement with Cuba. Further developments in 2015 resulted in embassies being re-established in the respective countries. In March 2016, for the first time in eighty years, a US president visited Cuba.

There was much speculation about possible outcomes. Would there be a tourist boom, an end to the US embargo, human rights improvements, freer travel, and improved employment and living conditions? Or would the result be just another Starbucks on every corner? Or perhaps this new Cuban spring would come to nothing.

It seemed to me the moment was right to record aspects of Cuba that could, in the near future, fade away or be gone forever; an opportunity to take a snapshot in that hiatus, “before the Americans returned.” If past history is any guide there will be no radical transformation, but the scent of change is in the air. Cuba is poised to move into another chapter of its fascinating five-hundred-year evolution.

INTRODUCTION

Most people I meet seem to want to visit Cuba. They imagine themselves cruising down the Malecón—Havana's seaside promenade—in an open-topped 1952 Buick Special Deluxe, the dusk light washing gold over the magnificent derelict buildings. The humid sea breeze is blowing in their hair and perhaps there is a Cohiba cigar in one hand and the other hand is tapping to the salsa beat of the Buena Vista Social Club playing on the crackly car radio. They think of Fidel Castro, Che Guevara, the Cuban Missile Crisis, and sipping a mojito at some bar made famous by Ernest Hemingway. Lately they may have heard that the decades-old time capsule is about to burst open as the famously cold relationship with the world, and particularly the USA, begins to thaw.

Although this clichéd rendition of Cuba is real, it is only one glossy part of a larger, more complex, and less enchanting picture. Looking at the decaying, crumbling architecture, you wonder how did comparable cities like Rome and Barcelona survive the centuries, yet Havana did not? You ride in gorgeous, creaky American cars, but question the small number of new cars on the streets. Around the idyllic countryside you are puzzled that they still use oxen and horses and carts. In the towns and villages you adore the colorful colonial villas and

Cruising the Malecón at sunset.

splendid Spanish churches, but speculate on how they have managed to remain intact, untroubled by modern development. You savor the unspoiled beaches and sheltered harbors guarded by awesome stone castles as yet not over-run by hordes of selfie-stick wielding tourists. You enjoy the marvelous music, the fabulous costumes, the intoxicating drinks and cigars, and above all the friendly, stoic people, and hope nothing changes.

Here, delving into the five-hundred-year story of Cuba with its indigenous tribes, conquistadors, pirates, slaves, booms and busts, wars of independence, foreign incursions, dictatorships, and revolution and desolation, you may gain a better insight into the remarkable island of Cuba.

The Cayo Santa Maria is a string of tiny islands connected by bridges and causeways extending thirty miles out into the Atlantic Ocean from the north coast of Villa Clara province. The pristine beaches include the Playa Perla Blanca, situated at the eastern end.

CHAPTER 1

Island in the Stream

You cross the soft white sand and are immersed in the clear, warm turquoise waters lapping the shore of the long curved beach. The palm trees swaying in the languorous breeze cast mottled shadows across your sun lounge and towel. You delight in the relief from the humidity and heat, and for a moment you contemplate the pristine, empty landscape and consider how it was five centuries ago, when the first Europeans approached these shores.

In January 1492, the Moors, after seven hundred years of rule, were finally driven out of Spain by Queen Isabella I and King Ferdinand II. Jealous of neighboring Portugal's global expansion, they sought a strategy to expand their economic and Christian influence. The eastern land route to India and beyond was blocked by the Ottoman Empire, so the idea of a western route was floated. After knock-backs

The Cruz de la Parra, in the Catedral de Nuestra Señora de la Asunción in Baracoa, is one of the twenty-nine crucifixes reportedly brought to Cuba by Christopher Columbus in 1492. Testing has shown that the wood is more than five hundred years old; as it was sourced from locally grown trees, it is unlikely to have come from Spain.

from the Portuguese, the Genoese seaman, Christopher Columbus, convinced the Spanish monarchs to finance his adventure to find a new route to the Indies.

The fleet of the *La Niña*, *La Pinta*, and *La Santa Maria* set sail from Spain on August 3, 1492, and made the first and famous discovery of land on October 12, near the Bahamas.

Just two weeks later, on October 27, 1492, Columbus first sighted Cuba. "This island is the most beautiful that eyes have seen, full of good harbors and deep rivers, and the sea appeared as if it never rose," exclaimed Columbus, as recorded in the notes of Fray Bartolomé de la Casas, known as the "Protector" of the Indians.

Baracoa fishermen work their nets near the Cuban coast first seen by Columbus in 1492.

In the indigenous language the word *taino* meant "peace."

Admiral Columbus was very pleased with his discovery and gave the name Juana to the island, in honor of Prince Juan, the only son of his sponsors Ferdinand and Isabella. From his charts, Columbus believed he had found Japan, but looked in vain for any signs of Oriental civilizations or the famed palaces made of gold. Instead he found the naked, friendly indigenous people, who became known as the Taino.

The Tainos, originally from South America, had occupied Cuba for just a few hundred years, supplanting the Siboney people and the Guanahacabibes before them. When Columbus arrived, the Tainos were under threat by the warlike Carib tribes, described by the Europeans as fierce, cannibalistic people. The Taino people in Cuba had a formal social structure and lived in small villages of well-made thatched huts called *bohios*, which survive today stylistically in the rural areas of Cuba. They cultivated corn, sweet potatoes, made a sort of bread from Yucca root, spun and wove cotton, and made pottery.

In time, Columbus came to believe that the north coast of Cuba was not Japan, but the Chinese mainland, and when the natives described a large town inland ruled by a powerful *cacique* (chief), he assumed this must be an important city like Quinsay, as described by Marco Polo. The exploration party he sent found a village of about fifty huts, but no gold and no Grand Khan. They did notice that the people carried firebrands and herbs rolled into tubes called *tobacos*. Later it was noted in the writings of Fray la Casas that, "these herbs gave a soothing effect, almost intoxication and relieved them from weariness."

Columbus went on to claim the nearby island he named Hispaniola (now Haiti and the Dominican Republic) and returned to Spain to a hero's welcome. He made several return voyages to the Caribbean without dispelling his notion that this territory was part of mainland China. It would take Sebastián de Ocampo's circumnavigation in 1508 to establish Cuba as an island.

Even after his death in 1506 Columbus continued to travel. First from Valladolid, Spain, his body was transferred to Hispaniola. Then, when the French invaded in 1795, he was moved to Havana. Finally, when the Spanish exited Cuba in 1898, he returned to Spain. Christopher Columbus never made it to America.

His son, Diego, who became governor of Hispaniola, then commissioned Diego Velásquez de Cuéllar to annex the island of Cuba to Spain.

In the garden courtyard of the Palacio de los Capitanes Generales, Havana Vieja, is a statue of Christopher Columbus framed by two Royal Palms. Seen everywhere on the island, they are not just the national tree, but to many Cubans these stately palms represent the power of the gods.

Santiago de Cuba's Casa de Diego Velásquez is considered the oldest residence in Cuba. It was constructed for the colony's first governor in 1530. It is a wonderful example of a *Mudéjar*-style house with its central courtyard, wooden screens, frescoes, and geometric ceilings called *alfarjes*.

An old barn near La Palma, Pinar del Rio province.

The Autopista Nacional de Cuba extends for more than five hundred miles, connecting Havana, the capital, in the northwest to Santiago de Cuba, the second city, in the southeast.

A farmer works with his oxen at dawn in the shadow of the Sierra la Guarsara. The limestone outcrops, called *mogotes*, dominate the landscape in the rich farmland of the Viñales area, in the western province of Pinar del Rio. Farmers in this area grow a range of produce, including sugar cane, bananas, mangoes, coffee, and tobacco.

B
20459

A tobacco farmer attends his crop near Viñales. The thatched hut, used for drying and curing tobacco, is known as a *casa de tabaco*. Its form derives from the original houses, *bohios,* built by indigenous people.

Sunday morning traffic on the road from Cienfuegos to Playa Rancho Luna, a popular beach for locals.

P132 342

The Real Fábrica de Tabacos Partagás, in Centro Habana, is the largest cigar factory in Cuba. It was founded in 1845, and produces twelve cigar brands, including Cohiba, Monte Cristo, and Romeo y Julieta.

A quiet country road in the Pinar del Rio region with a 1952 Chevrolet Styleline De Luxe sedan, one of Cuba's most popular cars of the pre-revolutionary era.

In the Plaza de San Francisco, Habana Vieja, outside the Basilica Menor de San Francisco de Asis, is the statue of Junipero Serra, who was a Catholic priest and friar best known for establishing a mission in Baja, California, in the eighteenth century.

CHAPTER 2

The Reign of Spain

You climb a dirt track winding its broken way up a hill that overlooks the old town. Beside a waste treatment plant stands the remains of a church with the impressive name Ermita de Nuestra Señora de la Candelaria de la Popa del Barco. It was built in 1740, about halfway through the four-hundred-year Spanish occupation of Cuba. The neglected ruin stands conceivably as a monument to the conquistadors' least successful attempt to establish another strong Christian outpost in the New World. First, the Afro-Cuban religions diluted the impact of the Catholic faith, and finally the Marxist Revolution promoted an atheist state.

In the fifteenth century, Spanish motivations for conquering the New World were to claim territory, find gold and other riches, and spread the word of their Christian god. They wasted no time after the discoveries by Columbus and began the colonization of Cuba by Conquistador Diego Velásquez in 1511.

The Museo de la Lucha Contra Banditos—previously the Iglesia and Convento de San Francisco de Asis in Trinidad. In the 1960s, the bell tower was used to look out for counter-revolutionary "bandits" who opposed the new Castro regime.

He landed with three hundred soldiers near the eastern tip of the island and founded Baracoa, the first permanent settlement. Six other settlements were established across the island: San Salvador de Bayamo (Bayamo) in 1513; San Cristóbal (Havana), Villa de la Santísima Trinidad (Trinidad), and Sancti Spiritus in 1514; and Santiago de Cuba and Santa Maria del Puerto de Principe (Camagüey) in 1515.

Hatuey, a Taino warrior and chief, traveled from nearby Hispaniola to warn his people of the danger of the invaders. He showed them a basket of gold and jewels, saying:

Here is the God the Spaniards worship. For these they fight and kill; for these they persecute us and that is why we have to throw them into the sea. They tell us, these tyrants, that they adore a God of peace and equality, and yet they usurp our land and make us their slaves. They speak to us of an immortal soul and of their eternal rewards and punishments and yet they rob our belongings, seduce our women, violate our daughters. Incapable of matching us in valor, these cowards cover themselves with iron that our weapons cannot break.

The native Taino did not heed his warnings and were brutally crushed by the Spanish, with their superior weapons, horses, and dogs. Hatuey fought valiantly against the conquistadors, but was eventually captured in 1512 and tried as a heretic. A priest asked him if he would accept Jesus and go to heaven. Hatuey, thinking a little, asked the religious man if Spaniards went to heaven. The religious man answered yes. The chief then said without further thought that he did not want to go there but to hell, so as not to be where they were and where he would not see such cruel people. He was burned at the stake.

By 1515, the entire island was conquered by the Spanish, with Velásquez the governor. The native population was decimated. Those that survived the massacres were killed by diseases like smallpox, measles, typhus, and influenza, while others were enslaved or driven into hiding. Velásquez's efforts to end the abuse of the Indians by use of *encomiendas*—a Spanish legal dependency device that ostensibly traded "protection" for service, but was really a cynical ploy to enslave them—were unsuccessful, and from 1527, the colonists were forced to import slaves from Africa to work their farms. By then, roughly five thousand out of a hundred thousand of the original Taino were still alive. Soon they would all be gone.

The Spanish found little gold or other easy spoils in Cuba and moved away to the more lucrative looting of Mexico and Peru. The remaining settlers took advantage of the vast plains and rolling hills blessed with rich soils watered by warm tropical rain. They raised cattle, tobacco, coffee, and small amounts of sugar cane and exported leather and hides.

Facing the Catedral de Nuestra Señora de la Asunción in Baracoa is the statue of Hatuey. It is inscribed: *Primer rebelde de America imolada en Yara de Baracoa* (America's first rebel burned in Yara, Baracao).

Havana's La Catedral de la Virgen María de la Concepción Inmaculada was described by Cuban poet Alejo Carpentier as "music set in stone." The elaborate Baroque facade incorporates the unusual feature of a pair of asymmetrical bell towers. The ashes of Christopher Columbus were said to have been kept there until the Spanish departed in 1898.

Trinidad prospered from trade in sugar and slaves for hundreds of years, but from the mid-nineteenth century it went into decline. This period of isolation gifted the legacy of a town retaining its original character untouched by modernization. It was declared a UNESCO Heritage Site in 1988, and has become a popular tourist destination. Despite this, the town remains a genuine home and community for ordinary Cubans and their families.

The seat of government, Baracoa, cut off by its remote location, was replaced by Santiago de Cuba, which in turn was replaced by Havana as capital in 1607. These towns, with their large natural harbors, grew in importance as strategic bases for the empire. They prospered from shipbuilding, as trading centers for the region, and most importantly as staging posts for the Spanish fleets arriving from Spain and returning home laden with their New World treasure.

By royal decree in 1513, there were *instructiones* specifying town planning requirements for all of the Spanish Empire. There followed the Laws of the Indies in 1573, which were a guide for the placement of streets, their orientation, the provision of a central plaza for social, economic, and military uses, and the site of a church. Unlike the British, French, Dutch, and other colonial rivals, Spain established well-designed and functional urban environments.

In the UNESCO World Heritage town of Trinidad you appreciate these pastel-colored buildings, their decorative grilles and moldings. As you explore the grid of cobblestoned streets punctuated by spacious squares and imposing churches you value this fine legacy of the Spanish occupation.

The view of the town of Trinidad, established in 1514, seen from the bell tower of the Museo de la Lucha Contra Banditos.

LA SANTISIMA

A 1957 Ford Fairlane 500 is parked on a Trinidad street paved with original irregular river stones called *chinas pelonas*.

A schoolgirl and her doll stand in front of the steel window grilles known as *barrotes*, which in nineteenth-century Trinidad replaced the carved wooden versions.

The Casa de los Sanchez Iznaga, with its red tiled roof, distinctive wall decorations, large wooden doors, and windows with *barrotes* exhibits all the key features of the Spanish colonial style.

The Iglesia de Santa Ana, on the eastern side of Trinidad, was built in the eighteenth century and remains unrestored.

This knowledgeable staff member at the Museo de Artes Decorativas, Santa Clara, wears quasi-traditional wardrobe that complements the *azulejos*-style tiled lower walls behind her desk.

The facade with distinctive arcades, balconies, and arched windows faces Havana's popular Plaza Vieja. This square was first laid out in 1559, and functioned as a market place and festival site. After suffering a recent incarnation as a car park, its more recent UNESCO Heritage status has seen it restored to a semblance of its original appearance. The colored glass half-moon shaped windows called *mediopunto* became popular in the eighteenth and nineteenth centuries.

A fisherman stands on the Castillo de San Salvador de la Punta, originally the western defense of Havana's harbor, when chains made of timber and brass rings floated across the opening to foul and block access to encroaching enemy vessels. Beyond is the El Morro fortress, which has become a representative symbol of the city of Havana.

CHAPTER 3

Pirates of the Caribbean

It is sunset, and you join the thousands of *Habaneros* gathered at the water's edge to take in the glorious panoramic view from Havana's Malecón. The western end is framed by the stark 1950s high rises of Vedado, while the eastern end is dominated by the picturesque, ancient profile of the El Morro fortifications. Names like Jack Sparrow, Long John Silver, and Captain Hook possibly do not spring to mind as you regard this benign looking rock solid fortress, yet those swashbuckling figments of the imagination were inspired by the real pirates of the Caribbean. These cruel and vicious sea dogs not only plundered the treasure ships across the seas of the Spanish Main, but also struck fear and trepidation into the town folk and villagers all around Cuba.

When the Spanish conquistadors realized Cuba was not endowed with easy spoils like gold and silver or other valuables they moved on to exploit the vast riches found in Mexico and Peru. Cuba, with its modest farming activities, was left to become the ugly duckling of the Spanish possessions. It was not too long before its strategic geographic location brought it back into favor.

Ships sailing from Spain were carried westward on the trade winds toward the eastern port of Santiago de Cuba, where they stopped for supplies. More importantly, the treasure-laden fleets, the *Flota de Indias*, that traveled east from Mexico and Peru assembled in Havana's spacious protected harbor. Even riches from the Manila galleons, which had sailed all the way across the Pacific from the Philippines and crossed the Panama isthmus overland by mule, were brought to join the fleet. Once all the ships were ready they embarked on the perilous journey across the Atlantic Ocean, taking advantage of the Gulf Stream to propel them toward Cádiz and Seville in Spain. This annual voyage in autumn might involve more than a hundred ships, accompanied and guarded by well-armed Spanish naval vessels.

Wars and alliances ebbed and flowed between the various European powers in the sixteenth and seventeenth centuries. France, Britain, and the Dutch were all from time to time at war with Spain. These countries were also jealous of Spain's conquests and possessions in the Americas and sought to right the imbalance by not only taking control of various territories in the region, but also by raiding the Spanish treasure gal-

The Castillo de la Real Fuerza was built in 1577. It was Havana's first significant military construction and replaced the original fort that was destroyed by rampaging buccaneers. Unfortunately, as it was set back too far from the harbor, it proved to be ineffective in defending Havana and eventually became a residence for governors and other highly ranked officials.

leons. The governments achieved this indirectly by commissioning privateers or corsairs to engage in these attacks. These seagoing mercenaries were awarded Letters of Marque which gave them official permission to attack foreign ships, with agreements to return a percentage of their winnings to their sponsor governments.

In addition to these "official" pirates there were various freelance operatives roaming the Antilles engaged in the same bloodthirsty incursions on shipping and towns, especially on the coasts. Among these were the buccaneers—originally French outlaws from Hispaniola who hunted cattle and pigs and learned from the Indians the process of drying meat and making bacon. These *boucaniers* first attacked the Spanish with canoes and light sea craft, and as they grew in force they graduated to larger vessels. Other raiders were called filibusters and free booters.

Together we know them as the dreaded pirates of the Caribbean, proudly flying their trademark skull and crossbones. Originally the flags were red, as this was considered more fearsome. The French, with a touch of irony, called their red ensign *Le Jolie Rouge*. The British, hearing this phrase, made it their own and called their flag the "Jolly Roger."

The pirates not only attacked the rich Spanish fleets at sea or moored in port, but also marched inland and attacked cattle farms and sugar plantations, and raped and pillaged towns and villages. Most of Cuba's first settlements were attacked from the 1530s onward, and while there

The view of Havana from San Carlos de la Cabaña, the largest defensive installation in Latin America. This fortress was built after the British invasion of 1762. Later it became a prison, and two centuries on was the notorious site of the many executions in the aftermath of the revolution.

El Castillo del Morro San Pedro de la Roca was finished in 1639. Originally it guarded the entrance to the Bahia de Santiago de Cuba from pirate attacks until 1775, when it became a prison. It saw service again during the Spanish-American war of 1898, defending the bay from the attack of the US fleet. The fortress contains the Museo de Pirateria.

The Malecón, with the Castillo de Los Tres Reyes de Morro beyond, is a prime spot for happy snaps. El Morro was the harbor's eastern defense, and in past times its cannons were discharged at day's end to signify the closing of the city's gates. Now they can be found in service as bollards in the streets of old Havana.

was some resistance from local settlers and Indians, they were no match for the superior fire power of the pirates. The town Camagüey, formerly Puerto de Principe, was built with narrow winding streets laid out in random maze patterns designed to prevent and confuse further attacks. This had mixed success, with the English buccaneer Henry Morgan occupying the city for several days. The town Remedios was moved inland twice to escape the attacks.

The sacking of Havana by French corsair Jacques de Sores in 1555 was to trigger a more concerted response by the Spanish government over the next hundred years. They set about building massive fortifications to protect the entrances to their principal ports: the Castillo de la Real Fuerza and Castillo de Los Tres Reyes de Morro in Havana, and El Castillo del Morro San Pedro de la Roca in Santiago de Cuba. Eventually all of the harbors of Cuba were defended by similar substantial battlements.

A fleet of thirty-six Dutch privateers led by Piet Heyn intercepted the annual Spanish *flota* off Havana in 1627. The Spanish were driven into the nearby Bay of Matanzas and forced to surrender. The Dutch returned home with booty valued at more than seven billion dollars in today's money. This loss in the midst of their wars in Europe contributed to Spain's relegation as a world power and loosened its stronghold on its colonies in the Americas. Conversely, the Dutch became stronger.

By the late 1600s, various treaties between Spain and the British, French, and Dutch put an end to hostilities and resulted in mutual recognition of their respective territories, ending much of the government backed piracy. In addition, by this time most of the Cuban ports had built formidable fortifications that

In the sixteenth century, the belfry of the Basilica Menor de San Francisco de Asis was used to keep watch for the approach of pirates.

made incursions into their harbors almost impossible. Nonetheless, the "freelancers" persevered and the golden age of piracy continued into the 1720s. Cuban pirates, with considerable help from their land-based mayors and governors, were still attacking US shipping as late as the 1830s.

Sailors, and particularly pirates, have become synonymous with rum. Sailing the long hauls across the Atlantic Ocean, it was found that alcoholic drinks would last longer and stay fresher than water, which became stagnant. The British had long used brandy for this purpose, but the war with the French cut off their supplies, so they swapped to rum, which was being produced in their colonies like Barbados and Jamaica. No doubt the intoxicating effects of these medicinal substances also enhanced their popularity.

Understandably, a large number of the slaves imprisoned on plantations and forced to toil in the cane fields and sugar mills refused to ingest the very product that was responsible for their misery-filled existence. Yet the Africans first distilled a spirit called

The nave of the Basilica Menor de San Francisco de Asis in Havana. It was originally a Catholic church, but during the British occupation of 1762 it was used by Protestants. With the return of the Spanish it never again functioned as a church and now serves as a chamber music concert hall.

cachaca from unprocessed cane juice. Later it was discovered that molasses, a by-product of the sugar refining process, could be fermented into alcohol. Further distillation and purification methods led to the creation of the first crude drink called Kill-Devil, until it finally became known as rum. For a time it was principally the drink of slaves, but was soon embraced enthusiastically by pirates and other seamen who took it from the Americas to the wider world.

By the 1830s, distillation methods became more sophisticated and rum evolved in to a more refined drink. Over the next hundred years Cuba became renowned for producing rum, and its famous rum-based cocktails the mojito, the cuba libre, and the daiquiri. One of the most successful producers was the Bacardi family in Santiago de Cuba, who started in 1862. Bacardi moved its operations to Puerto Rico in the 1950s, possibly anticipating the nationalization of their Cuban assets in 1960.

". . .Yo ho ho and a bottle of rum!" –Robert Louis Stevenson, *Treasure Island*

Prohibido
Pescar
sin
TOMAR

On the edge of the old city are remnants of Havana's sixteenth-century defensive walls.

The tiny island of Cayo Granma is home to a picturesque fishing village situated in the shadow of the El Morro fortress in the Bahia de Santiago de Cuba.

A contemporary coffee shop facing the Plaza del Cristo in La Habana Vieja.

CHAPTER 4

Azúcar Negra

You are sitting in a small café in Havana and the Afro-Cuban woman who has made you a delicious locally sourced cup of Cuban coffee passes you the sugar, maybe unaware of its inextricable link with her forebears. Little do you realize that five hundred years ago, apart from the taste of honey, it is unlikely this "sweet poison" would have passed your lips. Nor could you have imagined back then that this rare and valued delicacy would be reviled as a source of heart disease and obesity.

Sugar originated in New Guinea, and over time found its way to India and China. Arab traders brought it to the Mediterranean, where it was cultivated with limited success in Morocco, Palestine, and Sicily. Such was the attraction of this luxury product that they attempted cultivation even farther north in places like Tuscany. Greater success was achieved in the newly discovered Canary and Madeira Islands. Better still was the tropical climate of the West Indies. Cuba was perfect for growing sugar, being dominated by rolling plains, rich soil, and sufficient rainfall.

Sugar cane cuttings were brought from the Canary Islands to Cuba in 1512 by Columbus on his second voyage, yet for the next hundred years or so the sugar industry was secondary to cattle, tobacco farming, and the port commerce brought by treasure ships voyaging to and from Spain.

In the eighteenth century, the growth of sugar was boosted enormously during the brief rule of Cuba by the British in 1762–63. This interlude ended Spain's oppressive and monopolistic restrictions and immediately opened up trade with its Caribbean neighbors and Britain's burgeoning colonies in North America. That trade would flourish and remain Cuba's key source of income until the revolution two centuries later. There was a rapid transformation of Cuban society. Food, horses, and other goods flooded into the city, with the wealth reflected in the quality of the architecture. New cathedrals, mansions, administrative buildings, and town squares were created in a lavish fusion of Baroque, Moorish-Mudéjar, and Gothic styles.

Another event also boosted "King Sugar." Competition from the French colony St. Dominique evaporated with the slave revolt of 1791. The collapse of the dominant sugar industry in the island that would become Haiti sent French refugees fleeing to nearby Cuba. They brought enhanced sugar farming and milling expertise, money, and coffee. By the end of the next century, sugar would not only take over as Cuba's biggest industry, but Cuba would begin to dominate the world market.

Regrettably this growth would come at a human cost. Sugar was a labor intensive industry, and the response in Cuba, as elsewhere in the New World, was to utilize slaves. In the early 1500s, the Spanish sought to replace the indigenous Tainos by importing and exploiting people from the African continent. Africans were considered better workers

Farmers drive a pair of oxen and cart loaded with sugar cane.

and "four times stronger." The development of sugar caused transportation numbers to grow dramatically. In 1774, thirty thousand slaves came to the colony; in the next forty years that number would grow ten-fold. This brutal and nefarious trade resulted in a million slaves being taken to Cuba over the next hundred years.

Despite the gradual abolition of slavery throughout the Americas and a Spanish treaty with the British in 1817 to make the trade illegal, the real end to slavery in Cuba did not come until 1886, making it one of the last places on earth to officially end this brutal practice.

The Spanish were no better than anyone else and slaves suffered inhuman treatment. Worse than animals, they were literally worked to death in the barbaric sugar mills, with one in ten dying every year. Those who escaped were hunted down by dogs, and once recaptured were tortured mercilessly. They were brutally punished with floggings and ears sliced off. Many committed suicide by eating earth, taking poison, or hanging themselves rather than return to their living hell. In Havana, the colonial masters set up whipping houses where the more delicate owners could outsource their brutal punishment.

The victims of this evil trade came from various parts of Africa, including Senegal, Congo, Angola, Mozambique, and Nigeria. Their Spanish owners allowed slaves to retain their tribal associations in groups known as *cabildos*. These groups were able to continue their African cultural traditions, particularly their music and religious beliefs, which were woven together and inextricably linked.

Santería (*Regla de Ocha*) was developed by the Yoruba people from western Nigeria, with men called *Babalaô* appointed the priests of the cult. The *orishas*, who have human virtues and defects somewhat like the gods and goddesses of the Greeks and Catholic saints, are the intermediaries, indirectly enabling the veneration of the celestial empire. Unable to worship these figures openly before their Spanish Catholic masters, slaves secretly and cleverly linked many of their four hundred or so orishas to the various Catholic saints. Changó, the red god of war, virility, fire, thunder, and drums is linked with Santa Barbara. San Lazaru, who cures and heals, is known as Babalú Aye. The Virgen de Regla is assigned Yemayá, the sea goddess.

The religious ceremonies include complex and lyrical songs, dances, and rhythms using instruments like the conical batá drums. Dances like the rumba have evolved from these rituals, and so too the accompanying music has found its way deep into the DNA of Afro-Cuban culture.

Another significant cult is Palo Monte, also called *brujeria*, which means witchcraft. It came from the African Congo, and like Santería, it also cloaks its gods in the names of Roman Catholic saints. Santa Barbara is now Zaraban-

A grotesque drum displayed at the Museo Histórico de Guanabacoa. It is one of the kind said to be used by the Abakuá brotherhood during their funeral rites.

A singer at the performance venue attached to the Arieto Recording Studios in Centro Habana. Cuban musicians on the Egrem label (like the Buena Vista Social Club) have recorded at these studios since the 1960s.

da, the god of war and iron. This sect has the greatest influence on Cuban music and its intricate rhythms can be linked to the mambo, conga, and son.

Less popular and more secret is the all male Abakuá sect, which is popularly feared and compared to the voodoo sects of Haiti. Their complex hieroglyphics incorporate crosses, circles, and crossed lines. Their "little devils" (*biremes*) are seen manifested by dancers dressed in their image and have become a popular expression of Cuban folklore. Because of their secretive nature and death rituals the members of the sect have been convenient suspects and scapegoats for unsolved murders and disappearances.

"Abakuá will last in Cuba as long as there are drums."

This melting pot of history serves up many a spicy dish. From the blood, sweat, and tears of the monstrous slave trade has come the potent cultural legacy that embodies the unique Cuban experience, not just the vibrant Afro-Cuban demographic of the island's people, but the delightful diverse mash-up that is Cuban music.

Originally developed from a blending of Spanish melodies with West African rhythms, the music was

Adelaida tells fortunes in La Habana Vieja. Her decorations are adorned with some of the strange and mysterious symbols and signs associated with the syncretic religions, especially Abakuá.

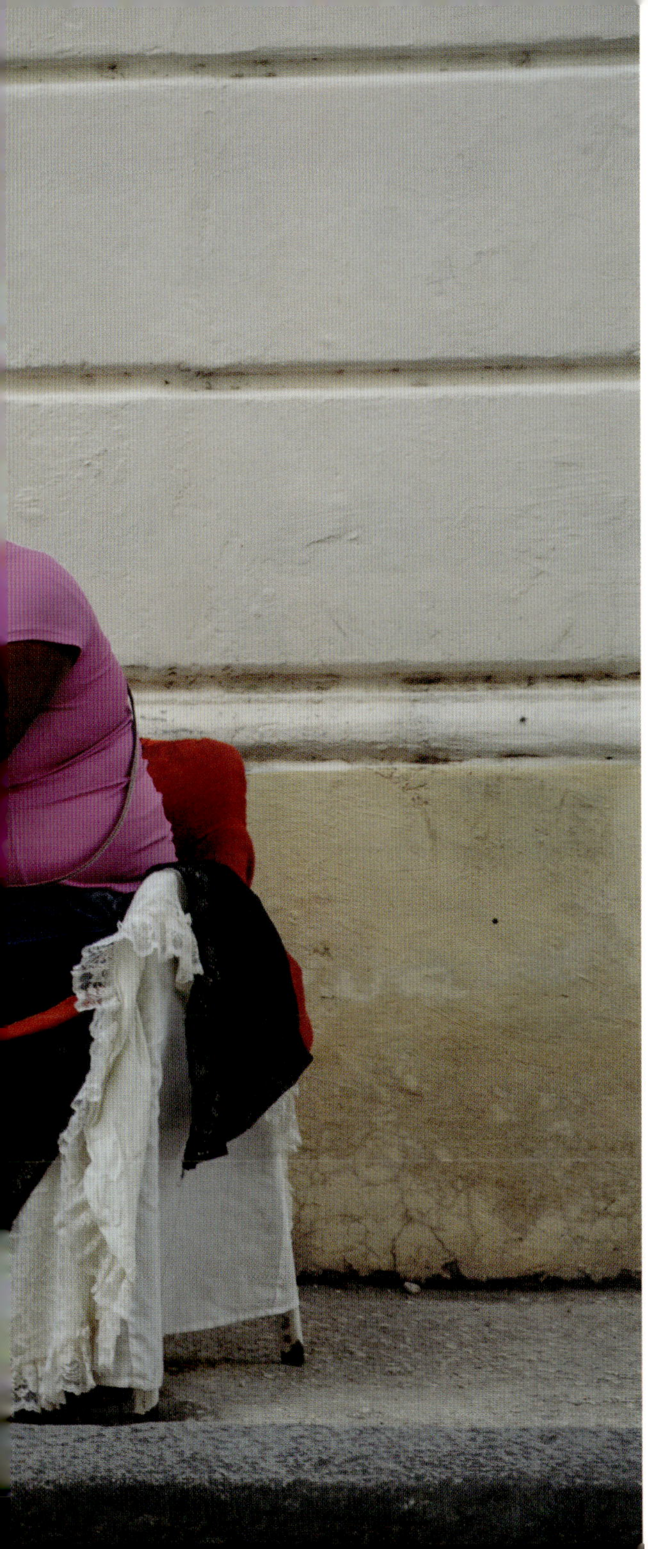

The black Madonna in the Museo Histórico de Guanabacoa.

further enriched by French Creole influences that came from Haiti. Maracas from the indigenous tribes, guitars from Spain, sticks and drums from Africa, and European instruments like the double bass and trumpet are all utilized in a wide range of combinations. And the Cubans added their own creations like the bongó and tumbadora drums, the tres and requinto guitars, the claves, the güiro gourd, and the merimbula piano. Jazz found its way to Cuba from America and then returned courtesy of Xavier Cugat and others in the 1930s. A good number of popular dances were associated with the music: rumba, cha cha cha, conga, mambo, and more recently the salsa.

Azúcar Negra was the signature song written and performed by Celia Cruz, the "Queen of Salsa."

A performer at the Casa de la Trova in Santiago de Cuba plays for the annual International Pepe Sánchez Trova Festival, named in honor of Sanchez, the father of the Latin Amercian Bolero and pioneer of the *trova* music style.

Patrons on the upstairs balcony at the Casa de la Trova, Santiago de Cuba.

A 1946 Chevrolet thunders through the rich plantations near Jamal, Guantánamo province.

Young dancers readying for a public performance in Santiago de Cuba's kilometer long shopping precinct know as *The Enramada.*

A musician arrives on Calle Heredia to perform at the Casa de Trova in Santiago de Cuba.

A *Santeras* (Santería priestess) poses outside the Iglesia de Nuestra Señora de la Virgen de Regla. Inside the main altar of this church can be found La Santísima Virgen de Regla, a black Madonna venerated in the Catholic faith and in Afro-Cuban Santería.

The statue of José Martí in the UNESCO World Heritage Parque José Martí, Cienfuegos, the "Pearl of the South." The city, established by French settlers in 1813, was laid out in a different, more formal fashion than Spanish settlements.

CHAPTER 5

Independencia o Muerte

Right from the beginning the Spanish colonists were precise and consistent in the planning of their settlements. They endowed each town and city with a central square or parade ground that became the focus of social and economic life. You may be relaxing in one such leafy park, with children playing, people sitting enjoying the sunshine, or lately individuals glued to their cell phones, taking advantage of a new wifi hotspot. You observe the gardens, the trees, park seats, perhaps a bandstand, and almost certainly a statue. In addition, you notice that each of these plazas has a name like Parque Martí, Parque Céspedes, Parque Vidal, Parque Maceo, or Parque Agramonte, and you find these names are repeated across the country, not only in parks and the statues, but street names, buildings, suburbs, and airports. You encounter these tragic commemorations in honor of the heroes of the nineteenth century who fought and died in the brutal and mostly futile wars for the independence of Cuba.

By the end of the eighteenth century, benefiting from the combination of increased slave labor and sugar production, the island had become economically strong. Middle class Cubans—both *peninsulares* and *creoles*—became wealthy, building well-planned towns with elaborate Baroque and neo-Classical buildings. There were regular steamship services, hundreds of miles of railways, street lighting, underground sewers, theatres, and port facilities. Havana in the 1820s was the biggest, flashiest city in the Caribbean. Rich Cubans even invested in their Spanish homeland's banks, cotton, and manufacturing.

In contrast, Spain, with the loss of income from its colonies and the impact of the Carlist wars, wallowed in economic depression and increasingly depended on Cuba as a market for exports and source of income. This subsequent constriction and monopolization of the island's economic freedom began to instill a desire to throw off the shackles of colonialism and become an independent nation. Cubans were also aware of the progress of their neighbors on the American mainland, where colonial rule was evaporating. The British had lost most of North America, and by 1824, Simon Bolivar and others had swept the Spanish conquerors out of Central and South America.

Nonetheless, for the first half of the nineteenth century, in spite of the discontent, injury, and sacrifice from decades of Spanish misrule, ever-faithful Cubans were not quite ready to go it alone. In 1817, out of a total population of just over half a million, more than three hundred thousand were African. The *criollos* and Spanish elite, with fresh memories of the 1791 slave revolt in Haiti and a series of local slave uprisings, feared the consequences of their own black rebellion. This suppressed their quest for independence to such an extent that it even induced a desire in some for the United States to take over the country.

By mid-century attitudes changed. More white immigrants came from Spain and from the newly independent South American states. More than a hundred thousand Chinese workers came, and the movement toward the abolition of slavery meant the importation of the people from Africa declined. By the 1860s, the proportion of slaves to whites was falling below fifty percent, reducing the fear of uprising. At the same time, as the country was the world's largest sugar producer, the wealthy Cubans had more of an incentive to escape from the tyranny and taxes of Spanish colonial rule.

The especially harsh rule of Spanish Governor Lersundi sparked the start of the Ten Years War. In the Oriente, on October 10, 1868, Carlos Manuel de

Blue is the favored color in the elegant Parque José Martí, which is flanked by the Antiguo Ayuntamiento, the Museo Provincial (formerly the Casino Espanol), and the El Palatino bar.

Céspedes freed the slaves from his estate. He called for an end to Spanish rule and the abolition of slavery. He was joined by uprisings led by Antoneo Maceo and Máximo Gómez. The smaller force of rebels was successful against the 250,000 Spanish troops brought to the island. Unfortunately for them the richer middle class, especially in the north, who cared more about preserving their exploitation of slaves, did not support the revolt. More than a quarter million Cubans died in the conflict, including Céspedes. Eventually it ended in a stalemate with the Pact of Zanjón in 1878. General Maceo rejected the agreement and was forced into exile. There were no real advances for the Cubans and the sugar industry was severely damaged. One positive outcome was the war's contribution to the end of slavery in 1886.

Another brief uprising came in 1879–80, and finally fighting resumed again on February 24, 1895, in Santiago de Cuba. This Second War of Independence was led by José Martí. Exiled since 1870 and residing in New York 1881–1895, this poet, political thinker, organizer, social activist, and romantic revolutionary inspired the independence cause with his writings. He formed the Cuban Independence Party in 1892, and over the next three years secured support for a new uprising with the military leadership of exiles General Maceo and Gómez. Tragically, Martí was killed right at the start of the war, at the Battle of Dos Rios on May 19, 1895.

The battles continued with Maceo and Gómez, and additionally Calixto Garcia. The rebel army was gradually liberating the entire island in spite of forces five times their size.

The Catedral de La Prisma Concepción, in Cienfuegos, built in 1833, with a Chevrolet Bel Air built in 1953.

P 119 841

General Maceo was killed in 1878, but Gómez struggled on with a war of attrition, torching a high proportion of sugar fields. The Spanish brought in General Weyler, whose famous counter-guerrilla strategy deprived the rebels of local support by imprisoning the populace into concentration camps, resulting in the deaths of one in ten people. Nonetheless, in spite of the cost to life and property, the rebels were on the brink of victory.

The US, fired up by newspaper reports of atrocities, sent the USS *Maine* into Havana harbor to "protect US interests." On February 15, 1898, the ship mysteriously exploded and sank. The US had their excuse to take action and declared war on Spain on April 25, 1898. The Cuban War of Independence had now become the Spanish American War.

The US had coveted Cuba for quite some time, with Thomas Jefferson offering to buy the island in 1808. After taking Florida from Spain in 1823, they again considered nearby Cuba should join them too. John Quincy Adams stated it was "a natural appendage of the North American continent." In 1853, President Franklin Pierce tried to buy the island from Spain for $100 million. To dispel a slew of fears among the Cubans of an American takeover, the Americans' declaration of war with Spain included the Teller Amendment:

A 1952 Buick Roadmaster Riviera convertible provides limousine services for the Hotel La Unión, founded in 1869 in Cienfuegos.

Dance rehearsals draw an audience outside the Casa Provincial de la Cultura (formerly the Palacio Ferrer), the grandiose residence of sugar baron José Ferrer. The Palacio was said to have hosted Enrico Caruso when he sang at the nearby Teatro Tomás Terry, Cienfuegos.

A stunning restored Spanish Baroque facade in Havana.

On the Avenida Belgica, Centro Habana, is the Palacio de las Ursilinas, with detailing modeled on the Mosque de Cordoba, Spain.

> The United States hereby disclaims any disposition or intention to exercise sovereignty, jurisdiction, or control over said island, except for pacification thereof, and asserts its determination, when that is accomplished, to leave the government and control of the island to its people.

A number of less convinced Cubans would recall José Martí's warning some years before: "And once the United States is in Cuba, who will drive them out?"

Calixto García's Cuban independence fighters combined with US forces, including Teddy Roosevelt's Rough Riders, overwhelmed the Spanish at the defining Battle of San Juan Hill. Days later, in the Battle of Santiago de Cuba, the Americans defeated the Spanish fleet and the war was over. It had lasted just four months. On December 10, 1898, the US and Spain signed the formal Treaty of Paris. Although the Cubans had participated in liberation efforts, the United States prevented Cuba from sending representatives to the Paris peace talks or signing the treaty. On January 1, 1899, Spanish governor Castellanos handed over the keys of Havana to US General Brooke and the flag of the United States of America now replaced that of Spain.

Modern dance practice in the Teatro de la Caridad in the Parque Vidal, Santa Clara.

A familiar combination in the streets of Havana: a broken down car and the ubiquitous Royal Poinciana, the tree that features in the 1936 song by Manuel Lliso called *La canción del arbol*, meaning "The song of the tree."

A 1950 Oldsmobile 88 is parked on a hilly street of colorful neo-Classical houses in Santiago de Cuba.

Historians often seem to focus on the politics and armed conflicts of the period and tend to ignore the other aspects of the time which have resulted in a more tangible legacy. You could view the nineteenth century in Cuba as a series of brutal, and in the end somewhat pointless wars for independence. Yet when you look at the beautifully crafted towns and cities, with their Baroque and neo-Classical architecture expressed not only in large public buildings, but also at the domestic level, you have a century that was booming sufficiently to be able to afford this high standard of building. The bones of modern Cuba were consolidated despite the destructive and bloody series of rebellions. And in spite of the last sixty years of neglect and abuse, this remarkable and rich architecture and infrastructure survives and contributes to the wonderful texture that is urban Cuba today.

Morning riders in Santa Clara.

The presidential palace was built in 1920, and remained the center of government until the 1960s, when it was turned into the Museo de la Revolución.

CHAPTER 6

Pseudo Republic

You would be forgiven if you found the political events of Cuba in the first half of the twentieth century confusing, colorless, and even boring; an era defined by a series of groundhog days involving a president or dictator coming or going, or both. There were minor skirmishes from time to time, simmering discontent, and the shadow of American influence in front of and behind the scenes. Still, as you stroll around the streets of Havana and encounter an amazing array of monuments, expansive plazas and grand boulevards, great public works, and dazzling Beaux Art, art nouveau, and art deco architecture, it is plain that Cuba was far from boring. You could argue that the projects were too ambitious and too expensive for a small country struggling with newfound independence. Undoubtedly they could have done more to eliminate poverty and other social ills, particularly with huge amounts of money ending up in the wrong pockets or traveling offshore. However, you could concede that these substantial developments exhibit a wonderful expression of hope and ambition for the future of a young republic. A self-belief that they dreamed it was possible to create a capital city and country on a scale and to a standard comparable with the great nations of the world.

The 1898 defeat of Spain was followed by four years of US occupation of Cuba. While the Americans sought to avoid being tagged neo-colonialists, their intentions were undermined by the terms of their subsequent imperialist legislation. The 1901 Platt Amendment was ostensibly aimed at maintaining peace on the island by way of US intervention, but it also allowed US supervision of Cuba's international trade and gave the US the long-term lease of Guantánamo Bay.

There was much jubilation with the establishment of the Republic of Cuba on May 20, 1902. US troops departed and Tomás Estrada Palma was proclaimed president. In 1906, there was an insurrection, and the US re-occupied the country until 1909, when José Miguel Gómez became the next president. He was followed by a string of leaders: Mario García Menocal (1913–1921), Alfredo Zayas (1921–1924), and 1924–1933, Dictator Gerardo Machado, the tropical Mussolini.

With the "Revolution of 1933" there came the rise to power of Sergeant Fulgencio Batista Zaldívar. His military coup was shrouded by the establishment of Dr. Ramón Grau San Martin as provisional president. Another five puppet presidents followed, then

A billboard in Guantánamo Province reads: "Welcome to Guantanamo First anti-imperialist Trench." The province famous for the notorious US base is also the home to that girl from Guantánamo enshrined in the song *Guantanamera*, written by Joselto Hernández, with some verses by José Martí.

The Gran Teatro hosted performances by luminaries like Sarah Bernhardt, Arthur Rubinstein, and Andre Segovia, and after the revolution became the home of the Alicia Alonso National Ballet.

The magnificent Gran Teatro de la Habana was formerly the elaborate Palacio del Centro Galligo. It was inaugurated in 1915 as a social club for Galician emigrants who came from northwest Spain, like Fidel Castro's forebears.

> They say that I was a terrible President of Cuba. That may be true. But I was the best President Cuba ever had.
>
> –Carlos Prío Socarrás

Batista took over as president in 1940. For a moment, with a new constitution and certain reforms, there was the slight chance that Cuba might move forward with a genuine democracy. However, Batista was replaced by Grau, who ruled again with the Auténticos Party until 1948, and was followed by Carlos Prío Socarrás.

The runner up at this election was Eduardo Chibás, from the Ortodoxos party, who out of frustration over chronic government corruption shot himself on live radio. One of his supporters was a young Fidel Castro, who would stand as candidate at the next election. Finally Batista returned from Florida, threw out Prio, and took control.

In spite of fifty years of governments prone to ineptitude, corruption, oppression, nepotism, and *gangsterismo*, Cuba experienced prosperity and growth, especially in sugar, tobacco, coffee, rum, and nickel. This economic prosperity was reflected in the development of the towns and cities and major pub-

lic works, like the construction of harbors, sewerage, and the central highway. It was also a period marked by an increase of imbalance between the rich cities and the dirt poor country. This schism would sow the seeds of discontent and later help fuel the hunger for Castro's revolution.

The Cuban economy was dominated by the USA, which monopolized almost every sphere of activity, from railways and shipping to electricity and telecommunications, and especially the sugar industry. The Americans also came as tourists, their numbers boosted in the 1920s prohibition era, when they rushed from their boats to take legal drinks at bars like Sloppy Joe's or Dos Hermanos near the port.

Escaping the US winter, they were also drawn by outdoor attractions like deep sea fishing, golf, polo, horse racing, and tennis. Gambling and other entertainments flourished and luxurious hotels like Hotel Nationale, Hotel Inglaterra, and Hotel Plaza attracted rich and famous guests like Isadora Duncan, Anna Palova, and Enrico Caruso. Room 511 of Hotel Ambos Mundos, built in 1924, was the home of Ernest Hemingway for about seven years and was where he wrote *For Whom the Bell Tolls*.

President Gerardo Machado built the iconic Capitolio Nacional. Modeled on the Pantheon in Paris, it is more commonly associated with the US Capitol, although it stands taller. The building cost more than twenty million dollars and bankrupted the treasury. Other major landmarks were constructed like the Prado, the Gran Teatro, the Presidential Palace, the national library, and a national museum. Elaborate art

The recently restored Gran Teatro is opposite Parque Central, which leads to the Paseo del Prado, the street in the early twentieth century that was home to Cuba's elite. This grand boulevard, with its fancy lamps, bronze lions, and marble benches, was designed by French landscape architect Jean Claude Nicolas Forestier.

The bus stop at Canasi, the former American company town Hershey built in 1917. It included schools, health facilities, and subsidized housing for the workers who operated the giant sugar processing facility.

La Bodeguita del Medio was transformed from a food shop into a bar in 1942. It is the legendary birthplace of the *mojito* and was a popular hangout for notable patrons like Pablo Neruda, Salvador Allende, Gabriel Garcia Marquez, and Ernest Hemingway, who lived at the nearby Ambos Mundos Hotel.

The Hershey electric train runs from Havana to Matanzas. This unique railroad was built in 1926 by the Hershey Corporation to link Havana's port at Casablanca to its once thriving sugar factory at Canasi, thirty miles east.

nouveau and art deco apartments and offices proliferated in the city. Americans started building the Malecón in 1901, and by 1923, the wide seaside avenue reached the mouth of the Almendares River, where the new fashionable suburbs of Vedado and Miramar expanded away from old Havana and the slums on the edges of the city.

The continued foreign investment, booming commercial enterprises, and corruption at all levels of government set the scene for the glamorous doom-laden final days of the Cuban Republic.

Coco cabs wait in front of the Hotel Nacional de Cuba, which was opened in 1930 by President Machado. It was the leading hotel in Havana until the arrival in the 1950s of the Riviera, Capri, and Hilton hotels. The infamous Mafia Summit was held here in 1946.

In 1837, Cuba became the first country in Latin America and the sixth in the world to build a rail network. Now the system is run down, with limited and unreliable service. It can take twenty hours to make the eight-hundred-mile trip from Havana to Santiago de Cuba. A train stands idle at the grand Estacion Centrale de Ferrocarriles, Habana. This imposing building was completed in 1912. Its troubled history started with disputes regarding the land it occupied and a subsequent duel to the death of a congressman. A hundred years later, decayed and disused, it is closed for restoration.

The landmark Edificio Bacardi, in Centro Habana, was designed by architect Esteban Rodríguez Castells. Inspired by the 1925 Exposition Internationale des Arts Décoratifs et Industriels Modernes in Paris, he incorporated the stylistic elements of art deco into the design of the building and its interiors. This was the headquarters of the world famous rum and spirits company, and when finished in 1930, it was Havana's biggest building.

In the early twentieth century the Barrio Chino was in its heyday, with cultural associations, theatres, and casinos. By the mid-twentieth century, Chinatown's reputation was less auspicious, with seedy clubs like the infamous Teatro Shanghai featured in Graham Greene's novel *Our Man in Havana*.

The western end of the Malecón culminates at the remnants of the harbor fortress known as the Castillo de San Salvador de la Punta.

The Malecón's official name is the Avenida de Maceo, named after Antonio Maceo, the "Bronze Titan." It has been called Havana's living room and is a popular place to hang out, swim, fish, take in the ocean views, and enjoy mojito sunsets.

The Malecón was designed by Cuban engineer Don Francisco de Albear in the late nineteenth century. The project was postponed by the Spanish government because of the high cost, but construction restarted in 1902, when the Americans took over.

The Hotel Habana Riviera, on the Vedado waterfront, was built in 1957 by mobster Meyer Lansky and was designed by architect Igor Polevitzky to rival the look and luxury of the latest Las Vegas hotels.

CHAPTER 7

Mid-century Mayhem

The glitter, girls, gamblers, and gangsters may be gone, but you can't miss the glamorous architecture of retro-Vedado and the old American cars roaming the streets. These crusty metal beasts with forgotten names like Desoto, Plymouth, and Studebaker still impress with their extravagant tail fins, chrome trimmings, and outrageous two-tone paint jobs in shades of pink and turquoise. They have become a popular symbol of Cuba to the outside world and one of the most visible reminders of the last decadent end of days, before the Cuban Revolution.

In the 1950s, Cuba had a booming economy that made it one of the most prosperous and advanced countries in Latin America. In spite of this, or because of this, there were uprisings, strikes, abortive attacks, and rumblings in the jungles of the Sierra Madre that were countered by the secret police torturing and killing suspects.

Leadership instability culminated in a military coup (*golpe*) in 1952. Fulgencio Batista abandoned his democratic ideals of the 1940s and established himself as dictator. Always with an eye on his personal wealth, he stimulated growth with graft friendly projects and the issuing of millions in bonds. Roads, civic buildings, hospitals, and schools were built. Cuba was now the world's largest sugar producer and also a major exporter of nickel and cobalt. It enjoyed the second highest per capita income in Latin America and was not far behind the USA in terms of life expectancy, doctors per capita, and other health indices. Poverty and conditions were markedly worse in the rural areas, although comparable with conditions experienced by the peasants of Spain, Italy, and Greece at that time.

Massive investment flooded in from the USA, both legitimate and not so legitimate. Batista encouraged tourism with tax breaks and government loans, and Cuba became the primary holiday destination for ordinary Americans, feted as the Las Vegas of the Caribbean. Movie stars and celebrities like Frank Sinatra, Ava Gardner, Errol Flynn, and Marilyn Monroe were seen at the clubs, casinos, and cabarets like the Tropicana, enjoying daiquiris and mojitos and dancing the mambo and the cha cha cha.

Now sufficient time has passed for the stunning untouched "retro" features of the Riviera to become fashionable again.

The Havana Hilton, with its tiled mural by Amelia Pelaez, was completed in 1958. Designed by architects Welton Becket & Associates, it opened as Latin America's tallest and largest hotel. Less than a year later it was taken over as the headquarters of Fidel Castro, then nationalized in 1960 and renamed the Habana Libre.

The Edificio FOCSA was designed by architects Ernesto Gomez Sampera and Martin Dominguez. It was the second tallest concrete building in the world when finished in 1956, and a testament to Cuba's engineering and construction eminence. It remains the tallest building in Havana.

The Instituto Cirugia Cardiovascular was built in 1958, and incorporates a voluptuous sculptural screen by Roland Lopez Dirube. The building is an appropriate period backdrop for the 1955 Chevrolet convertible.

> Stage and dance floor were open to the sky. Chorus girls paraded twenty feet up among the palm trees, while pink and mauve searchlights swept the floor. A man in bright blue evening clothes sang in Anglo-American about Paree.
>
> –Graham Greene, *Our Man in Havana*

The country was awash with the good times and the bad. Prostitution and seedy nightclubs like the Shanghai Theatre flourished. The National Lottery, the *bolita*, was immense. Counterintuitively, to create an "honest" gambling industry Batista invited businessmen experienced in managing Las Vegas casinos to come to Havana. Men like gangster Meyer Lansky accepted the invitation, expanding their operations with flashy new nightclubs and new hotels like the Capri and the Riviera dominating the

The Malecón was the setting for the 1958 Formula One Grand Prix, during which Juan Manuel Fangio, the world's number one racing driver, was kidnapped by the revolutionary 26th July Movement. He missed the race, but was unharmed, and did not express ill will toward his captors or their cause.

Quite out of character with its neighbors in the five-hundred-year-old town of Remedios is this perfectly preserved time capsule from 1950. The interior is similar in character, and there is a pristine 1956 Chevrolet in the garage.

On La Linea, one of the main thoroughfares of Vedado, is the Teatro Mella, named after the founder of the Cuban Communist Party, who was assassinated in 1927 in Mexico.

city skyline and useful as outlets for their money laundering and other illegal rackets.

Cubans in the cities embraced the American lifestyle and the US newspapers, radio, television, and other consumer goods. Cuba became the biggest importer of American cars. New suburbs sprung up with streets of split-level houses modeled on the latest US styles. Prestigious state of the art shopping centers were built like El Encato and Fin De Siglo.

Yet among the Cuban middle class and intellectuals, the familiarity with the American way of life and prosperity highlighted the chasm between the economies of the two countries. They could not ignore the vast difference between the wealth in the Cuban capital and the poverty in the countryside exacerbated by Batista-backed privileged labor unions. Graft and corruption had infected every part of the government, and there were increasingly higher taxes and growing unemployment. Ordinary people became more and more alarmed at the vice, the crime, and above all the barbaric and cruel repression by Batista's secret police.

The time was ripe for a new, honest, and democratic government that was there for all the people. A government like that promised by Fidel Castro.

Acapulco

> The long city lay spread along the open Atlantic; waves broke over the Aveneda de Maceo and misted the windscreens of cars. The pink, grey, yellow pillars of what had once been the aristocratic quarter were eroded like rocks; an ancient coat of arms, smudged and featureless, was set over the doorway of a shabby hotel, and the shutters of a night-club were varnished in bright crude colours to protect them from the salt and the sea. In the west the steel skyscrapers of the new town rose higher than lighthouses into the clear February sky. It was a city to visit, not a city to live in.

–Graham Greene, *Our Man in Havana*

A 1937 Chevrolet passes the 1950s Acapulco service station in Havana's Nuevo Vedado district. The suburb's surviving streets and houses look like something out of the pages of a 1950's *Home Beautiful* magazine.

The enduring legacy of the fabulous 1950s is epitomized by ever-present American automobiles like this collection of convertibles lined up in front of the Gran Teatro, Havana.

The stairway to the apartment featured in the acclaimed Cuban film *Fresa y Chocolate* (Strawberries and Chocolate), 1994, directed by Tomas Gutierrez Alea and Juan Carlos Tabio, is now entry to the landmark Havana restaurant La Guarida, situated at the top of this decrepit building.

CHAPTER 8

Revolución

Do you ever wonder if the legend of the Cuban Revolution would have endured quite as long without that iconic image of the charismatic "Che" Guevera captured by Alberto Korda in a 1959 photograph? The tourist areas of Cuba abound with souvenir green caps and berets, but most of all the ubiquitous T-shirts, key rings, coasters, and ashtrays—in fact, anything and everything is adorned with Che's face. All around the country there are faded hand painted murals and billboards that display more images and proclaim heroic quotes like, "Hasta la victoria siempre." There are more substantial reminders of the revolution like the squares, museums, and monuments that glorify key moments of the revolution and record the names of the pantheon of heroes. Yet these images seem like a distraction from the real legacy of the events of 1959, when you encounter the decaying houses and defunct buildings, empty shelves in shops, horse-drawn taxis on pot-holed roads, and the less visible angst and pain in the hearts and minds of the people.

Fidel Castro, the young middle class lawyer, stood for parliament in the 1952 elections as candidate for the Ortodoxos Party. Batista, struggling in the polls and unwilling to trust the democratic process, staged a military coup, cancelled the elections, and sacked President Prio, who joined a long line of earlier leaders and fled abroad. Frustrated by the inability of the courts to oust this "illegal government" of Batista, Castro launched his rebellion. Hoping the July festival in Santiago de Cuba would be a distraction, he attacked the Moncado Barracks with a force of 165 men on July 26, 1953. The action was a disaster, with seventy of his force killed and the remainder, including Castro and his brother Raúl, captured. At his trial Fidel Castro proclaimed his famous "La Historia Me Absolvera" (history will absolve me) speech and was sentenced to fifteen years in prison on the Island of Pines.

Seeking to validate his regime, Batista had himself re-elected "legitimately" as president in 1954. Then, in a decision that he no doubt came to regret, he felt sufficiently secure to magnanimously grant a general amnesty to all the political prisoners, including the Castro brothers. Forbidden from making public speeches in Cuba and fearing he would be imprisoned again, Castro departed for Mexico and the US in 1955. Under the banner of the 26th July Movement (M-26-7), he sought support and plotted the next move,

A 1960s card collector's album that tells the story of the revolution in comic book form.

The art deco Cuartel Moncado in Santiago de Cuba. The former army barracks is now a high school, but also houses the Museo Histórico 26 de Julio, complete with 1953 bullet holes reinstated in the exterior walls.

A light show commemorating the revolution plays upon the face of the Ayuntamiento in Santiago de Cuba. Fidel Castro made his victorious inaugural speech to the nation from this balcony on January 1, 1959. In December 2016, his ashes returned here before reaching their final resting place near that other Cuban hero, José Martí, in the Cementerio Santa Ifigenia.

A typical street in Habana Vieja with decayed walls enlivened by a colorful portrait of "Che."

The mural depicts the faces of revolutionary heroes Ernesto "Che" Guevara with trademark beret and star, Camilo Cienfuegos with wide brimmed hat, and Julio Mella. The Moncado Barracks, *Granma*, and Fidel have also been worked into the picture. Ironically, Fidel's dying wish was to prohibit any depiction of his image in public.

On T-shirts and all sorts of trinkets, even ashtrays and drink coasters, "Che" is just another product like Cuban rum and salsa.

assembling a band of revolutionaries, including his brother Raúl, Argentine physician Ernesto "Che" Guevara, and Cuban dissident José Antonio Echeverría.

In December 1956, Castro returned from Mexico with a band of just eighty-one comrades crowded on to the six-berth leaking cabin cruiser *Granma*. The boat was blown off course and shipwrecked. The coast guard and government troops subsequently attacked and killed all but fifteen of the rebels. The Castro brothers, "Che," and a handful of other survivors retreated into the dense Sierra Maestra mountains in the eastern part of Cuba known as the Oriente.

With the economy booming it was mainly young students and poor rural people who supported the rebels and instigated train derailments, power blackouts, bombings, and incendiary fires. Continuing terrorist activities culminated in 1957, in ill-fated attacks on the presidential palace and the Havana Radio Station by the Directorio and Autenticos parties. Leader José Echeverría was killed. With the communists joining the other urban groups in the fight against Batista, Castro feared competition for leadership. He therefore declared his commitment to "free, democratic elections" and convinced all parties of the rebel coalition to agree to put liberal

The Complejo Monumental Ernesto “Che” Guevara in Santa Clara includes a memorial and museum of “Che” and is the resting place of his remains.

Even the tiny island of Cayo Granma, near Santiago de Cuba, has an office of the Committee for the Defense of the Revolution (CDR) complete with a picture of *El Jefe.*

Trains still pass along the railroad tracks right beside the Monumento a la Toma del Tren Blindito, which honors "Che's" historic victory in Santa Clara.

judge Manual Urrutia Lleóa as head of any new government of Cuba.

President Batista responded to the attacks and strikes with increasingly repressive measures using his secret police, the Servicio de Inteligencia Militar. Reprisals were carried out with sufficient brutality that dissatisfaction and revulsion spread to all levels of Cuban society and abroad, with even the US government appearing to withdraw support. This growing hatred of Batista played into Castro's hands.

Counting on grass roots support, particularly from the landless farmers, the rebel forces holed up in the mountains had grown to two or three thousand. Batista launched an all-out offensive to finish Fidel, sending tens of thousands of troops to the Sierra Madre. This operation ended in the battalion's defeat and its commander joining the rebels. Emboldened by this success, Castro's forces came down from the mountains to launch their counter-offensives. "Che" led forces west toward the central province of Las Villas Camillo Cienfuegos, aimed for the western province of Pinar del Rio, and Castro moved toward Santiago de Cuba.

The legendary turning point came at the end of December 1958, with the Battle of Santa Clara. "Che"'s division uprooted the rail tracks using a Caterpillar bulldozer and a few tractors, disrupting the 10,000 government troops on board, severing the communication system of the country, and taking the city.

President Batista caught a flight to the Dominican Republic, and on New Years Day 1959, Cuba was without a head of state. "Che" and Cienfuegos marched on Havana and Castro took Santiago de Cuba. After a televised victory speech from the balcony overlooking the Parque Céspedes, Fidel Castro made a triumphant procession across the island from east to west, arriving in Havana on January 8.

Manuel Urrutia Lleóa had already been made president with José Miró Cardona appointed prime minister. Former Batista supporters and those among Castro's allies who objected to the brutal lurch away from democracy were rounded up and imprisoned or executed by firing squads presided over by "Che" Guevera. Castro remained head of the armed forces, very soon became prime minister, and by July 1959, El Comandante was in complete control. One Cuban dictator had been replaced by another.

The roof of the Iglesia de San Francisco de Asis, with its commanding view of the Sierra de Escambray, was used as a lookout for counter-revolutionary "bandits" who waged war against the Castro regime in the early 1960s.

Photoclub
FOTOGRAFÍA Y VIDEO
alta definición
fotografía
impresión
infotur
Todo por la
REVOLUCIÓN

The flag of the 26th July Movement flies at the monument to the Battle of Santa Clara situated atop the Loma del Capiro. This hill, with strategic views over the city and countryside, was used as "Che" Guevera's command center.

The faces of Mella, Guevera, and Cienfuegos feature on this iconic faded billboard on La Rampa in Vedado that was replaced by a fresher, updated, more colorful version just prior to the 2016 visit of US President Obama.

Sunset on the Malecón can be enjoyed from the balcony of the stylish Soviet-themed restaurant, Nazdarovie.

CHAPTER 9

Aftermath

It started off so well. The "people" had finally driven out their US-backed dictator. At last, after fifty years, Cubans felt they had a truly independent Cuban Republic and an opportunity to rebalance the inequality between the richer middle classes of the cities and the impoverished rural communities. The time had now come for an ideal society that provided education and health for all and included a reformed and fair farming sector. The popular revolutionaries, dominated by the M-26-7 Movement, were swept into power with the goodwill and hopes of all the populace. It just did not pan out as the people had wished.

The new revolutionary government immediately set out to eliminate illiteracy by sending students throughout the rural areas and building thousands of classrooms. To empower landless farmers agrarian reform was initiated by the abolition of large estates and their foreign ownership. Health care was nationalized and clinics were established everywhere, offering free medical aid and widespread vaccinations.

New roads and houses began construction and sanitation and water supplies improved. Sport and culture were actively encouraged and supported financially.

President Urrutia, who feared the swing of the government toward communism, was soon dispatched and Castro took complete control. Now there was no mention of the promised free elections because, "the revolution has no time to waste in such foolishness."

International and Cuban businesses large and small were nationalized. Private property was expropriated, as were utilities, infrastructure, and banking. The media was not only taken over by the government, but used as a tool for propaganda and control of the people. The Catholic church and other religions were shut down and homosexuals, rock and rollers, tourism, and any other symbols of "capitalist decadence" were outlawed or discouraged. Without trial, offenders were executed or imprisoned in the farm labor camps known as UMAP. Even Christmas was abolished. "Neighborhood watch" groups called Commitees for the Defense of the Revolution (CDR) were set up where citizens were encouraged to spy and report on any "counter-revolutionary" activities of their neighbors. By 1965, there were an estimated 20,000 political prisoners in detention.

An increasing stream of professionals, middle class workers, and business people soon followed pro-Batista exiles out of Cuba. There was huge disappointment that they did not have their expected dem-

In 1957, the anti-government, anti-communist Student Revolutionary Directorate made an ill-fated attack on the presidential palace. After the overthrow of the Batista government in 1959, somewhat ironically, it was re-badged as the Museo de la Revolución.

COMITE DE
DEFENSA DE LA
REVOLUCION
609
611

ocratic government. Both within and out of Cuba there arose a desire for an end to this new totalitarian communist style regime. With the encouragement of the disaffected USA, which had seen billions of dollars of its investment shut down, Cuban exiles sought to overthrow Castro. The subsequent ill-fated Bay of Pigs invasion of April 1961, sealed the deal for an end to any continuing friendly dialogue between the US and Cuba, and set the course for decades of reproach and hatred from US-based Cuban exiles.

Fidel Castro, fearing the oncoming isolation, proclaimed aloud his embrace of Marxist-Leninist doctrines and ensconced his country within the sphere of the USSR. The Russians naturally liked the idea of a friendly Caribbean base so close to their Cold War enemy, the United States. What started with supply of arms and military assistance progressed to nuclear warheads and culminated in the Cuban Missile Crisis of October 1962, bringing the USA, the USSR, and the world to the brink of WWIII.

In spite of a settlement between the superpowers, Cuba's uncomfortable relationship with the USSR continued and prospered. The Cuban economy, struggling from the loss of industry and trade and the incompetence of its centralist administration, was relieved to be bolstered by the Russian Bear and its COMECOM satellites. The Cuban government had the means to move forward with its idealistic partly worthy, partly unrealistic socialist agenda. The government borrowed

A Comités de Defensa de la Revolución (CDR) in a back street of Havana.

and spent big on housing, schools, and hospitals, and encouraged the arts and sport, untroubled by the false sense of achievement and unconcerned at once more becoming the virtual colony of yet another superpower.

In spite of the death of "Che" in 1969 and with no encouragement from the Russians, Castro persisted with exporting the revolution abroad. Excursions to Latin America and African countries like Angola resulted in further public debt, the unnecessary loss of thousands of Cuban lives, and the subsequent branding of the country as a terrorist organization, engendering further isolation internationally.

It was not surprising that Cubans sought lives, careers, and futures elsewhere from a repressive state with no free speech, no free enterprise, and a stuttering economy kept afloat by the Soviets. The internal dissatisfaction resulted in more and more Cubans seeking to leave the country. Massive migrations ensued, like the Mariel boat lift which alone involved 125,000 people. By 1980, there were half a million Cubans living outside Cuba, and by 1993, this had risen to more than one million—roughly one in ten people.

The Alicia Alonso Ballet Company was established in 1948. The new revolutionary government of 1959 granted it much needed funding and it became the National Ballet of Cuba. Today it is recognized as one of the premiere ballet schools in the world, with students drawn from afar and as close as the USA.

Dance in classical and traditional forms is an intrinsic and joyous element in the education of Cuban children.

The pre-revolutionary Palacio Ferrer in Cienfuegos became a post-revolutionary community center.

Even with the example of Poland and other Russian satellites moving away from the socialist model and in spite of token toying with a market economy, no meaningful reform was forthcoming. There followed the Rectification of Errors and the subsequent rectification of the rectifications, meaning there would be no relaxation or retreat from the hard-boiled communist dogma. In the end, the events of Eastern Europe in the 1980s had no influence on Castro, who declared Cuba would sink before it sacrificed socialism.

Socialism or death.

–Fidel Castro

Street names were changed after the revolution, but unofficially many of the originals remain in place and continue to be used. This dual naming causes confusion to visitors and particularly users of GPS navigation devices.

Dominoes is often called Cuba's second national sport.

Youngsters practice boxing in a vacant lot in Habana Vieja, perhaps hopeful of following in the august footsteps of their world renowned Cuban predecessors like Teófilo Stevenson, Félix Savón, and Sardiñas Montalvo, a.k.a. Kid Chocolate.

The Sacra Catedral Ortodoxia Rusa was inaugurated in 2008 to serve the spiritual needs of the ten thousand Russians still residing in Havana. Next door is Dos Hermanos, better known for serving spirits to visiting Americans during the prohibition era of the 1920s.

Heading off to school in Trinidad by horse and cart.

Young students display their dancing prowess in a public performance in the center of Santiago de Cuba.

Derrumbe means collapse, and is the term used by Cubans to describe the situation where many of their decrepit buildings regularly fall down, often killing the occupants. The danger is exacerbated during heavy rains and wind.

CHAPTER 10

El Período Especial

Most people in eastern Europe in the early 1990s were pleased to say goodbye to Soviet automobiles like Ladas, Moskovitchs, Polski, and Vaz, not to mention seeing an end to the brutalist chunky Russian-style buildings polluting their landscapes. More importantly, they saw an end to the smothering influence of a totalitarian regime and Marxist-Leninist doctrines. Not so the Cubans; the departure of their communist friends was going to be painful.

When Mikhail Gorbachev became leader of the USSR in 1985, he saw his country's economy was struggling and its citizens were suffering from a poor standard of living and lack of freedom. He introduced dual solutions. *Perestroika* involved restructuring away from the centralized government concept toward a market driven economy and *glasnost* allowed greater freedom of media and religious and human rights.

Further reforms saw moves toward democratic elections, an end to the cold war and arms race, and the relinquishment of control over the Warsaw Pact countries.

Not only did the communist regimes fall in Poland, Hungary, East Germany, Czechoslovakia, Bulgaria, and Romania, but also by the end of 1991, the USSR had dissolved into fifteen individual republics. Suddenly Cuba's beneficial big brother was gone. The Soviet bloc had accounted for eighty-five percent of Cuba's trade. Now sugar was no longer purchased at artificially high prices and most significantly, the supply of bargain priced oil dried up. The Cuban economy shrank by seventy-five percent.

Cubans could not work in factories that had no electricity. There was no money to import goods or spare parts. Horses and bicycles replaced cars and buses. Tractors were replaced by mules and bullocks. Because crops had been destroyed in lieu of sugar and with the broken-down distribution of produce, food became scarce. Citizens were forced into long queues for rations of rice and beans. People were starving. Cats, dogs, and birds disappeared, including peacocks, buffalo, and rhea from the Havana Zoo. Hamburgers were made from banana peels and steaks from grapefruit rinds. Poor diet and vitamin deficiencies caused an epidemic of optic and peripheral neuropathy; fifty thousand people were going blind. There were harsher penalties for killing a cow than killing a human. There were no funds for new housing, nor even for the maintenance of existing structures.

The severe housing shortage forces people to inhabit pockets within the shells of buildings. With paint and other building materials expensive and in short supply scenes of neglect and decay are the norm.

MINERVA

Cuban farmers and cowboys are known as *guajiros*.

The embargo and scarcity of foreign currency has meant that ancient equipment remains in common use in repair shops and factories.

Fidel Castro, observing the unraveling of the Eastern Bloc countries, was not prepared to risk reforms of a similar kind in Cuba, instead eschewing "socialism or death." Unfortunately, many Cubans had no such choice, dying of starvation or committing suicide, or continuing the hazardous exodus out of the country, with scores drowning or being taken by sharks. By the early 1990s, even the hard line socialists were forced to make a handful of concessions that might help alleviate the crisis.

The government allowed food growers to sell their produce directly to the public in farmers' markets. Some of the people were allowed to engage in a prescribed list of about one hundred "free enterprise" businesses. Homeowners were permitted to serve meals to limited numbers of guests in *paladars* and to let out rooms known as *casa particulares*. The US dollar was legalized, and investment and joint ventures by foreign companies were encouraged, particularly in the establishment of holiday resorts. Moreover, in spite of its decadent capitalist connotations, tourism was embraced unconditionally, and by 1995, it was earning more income than sugar. Controversially, Cubans were not permitted to access the facilities and beaches used by tourists or savor the better food or services. This "tourist apartheid" made the Cubans second class citizens in their own country.

Thirty to forty percent of Cuba's housing is in poor condition or worse. Without plumbing in much of the city's habitation, water must be collected from government tankers. Vacant lots formed by collapsed buildings are strewn checkerboard-like across all of Havana.

Without spare parts or fuel, tractors are supplanted by horses and oxen, which remain in many rural areas as common as motor vehicles.

Bicitaxis, the Cuban "rickshaw," were introduced during the Special Period and remain an intrinsic component of transportation in Cuba.

Morning in Remedios and a fleet of bicitaxis heads off to work.

These small concessions and shifts toward a free market economy and a more liberal Cuba would not last. The government flirted with President Chavez swapping Cuban doctors and teachers for Venezuelan oil and other support. Other reforms were wound back. The US dollar was replaced by the convertible peso, the CUC. New licenses for paladars and casa particulares were curtailed. Joint ventures with foreign investors collapsed.

The shedding of state control by communist countries like Russia, China, Vietnam, and Soviet Bloc countries had little or no effect on the policies of Fidel Castro and his successor Raúl. Cuba would emerge from the difficult years of The Special Period in Time of Peace with only minor steps forward in its evolution.

China sold more than a million bicycles to Cuba in the early 1990s. These were then re-sold to the people at reduced prices.

Once one of the world's most sophisticated factories, the Hershey sugar factory is now a heartbreaking ruin. Nationalized in 1960, it survived thirty years courtesy of Soviet subsidies, but in 2003 it finally ground to a halt.

A *paladar* in Cienfuegos. The name *paladar* was taken from the name of a chain of fictional restaurants in *Vale Tudo*, a popular Brazilian TV soap opera.

Walking down the boulevard of broken dreams.

Trinidad's workers and school children set off early in the morning to avoid the daily heat and humidity. Diesel engines in tractors and cars lack emission controls and create smoky, polluted streets.

CHAPTER 11

New Millenium

A 1950s Chevrolet Bel Air sedan is parked in colorful contrast beside the crumbling ochre façade of a nineteenth-century neo-Classical building. This unlikely juxtaposition has become the definitive postcard image of Cuba today and underscores the enduring legacy of the Spanish and the Americans. Ironically, these very symbols of Cuba's colonial and capitalist past that the revolution sought to eliminate have inadvertently been preserved by the revolution and become the very elements that attract tourists and define Cuba internationally.

The small concessions and initiatives instigated to pull Cuba out of the dark days of the Special Period have not evolved since then to the degree one might desire or expect. There are empty roads and highways, abandoned factories, collapsed buildings, empty ports, dysfunctional railways, and people still riding horses, carts, and bicycles. Others crowd into old cars strung together with paint and wire, powered by diesel engines from Polish tractors or into the rear metal trays of tip trucks operating as buses. Drinking water is unreliable, as is the electricity supply, resulting in annoying *apagones* (blackouts).

The iniquitous dual currency continues to divide and eat away at this so-called classless society. There are more opportunities for self-employed people (*cuentapropistas*) and more casa particulares and paladars, but the state shops display empty shelves, people must still queue at pharmacies, banks, and health facilities, and many are forced to resort to black market goods and services to survive. Catholics and Protestants are no longer suppressed with the hosting of several Papal visits, yet the Afro-Cuban religions remain more popular. Literacy standards remain high and infant mortality rates and other health indices continue at impressive levels, but not at first world standards. There have been minimal changes to the political system, no relaxation of regime-controlled media, and this police state has zero tolerance of dissidents.

Since taking over from his ailing brother Fidel in 2006, Raúl Castro has shown himself to be pragmatic and results oriented in his approach to government. A variety of initiatives have been put in place aimed at a gradual progression to a freer market economy. Measures have been taken to decentralize the control of the government and its monopoly of all facets of the economy. Unprofitable state enterprises are

Modern locals are nonchalant about their remarkable daily lives amidst crumbling eighteenth- and nineteenth-century architecture and mid-twentieth-century motor vehicles.

At a market on the edge of Santa Clara the range and volume of produce is limited.

US Secretary of State John Kerry presided over a ceremony in August 2015, to reopen the US Embassy, with the stars and stripes raised in Cuba for the first time in fifty-four years. Nine months later posters heralded the visit of President Obama, the first visit by a US president since Calvin Coolidge in 1928.

Produce from small farms and markets is sold directly by street vendors.

being shut down and government workers transitioned into private companies. Cubans have been allowed to buy and sell their homes. A limited number of new resorts have been built and a selection of hotels refurbished to cater the increasing numbers of tourists. There are ATMs, limited internet services, and even wifi hot spots in the main plazas of towns. Historic monuments and heritage areas of towns and cities have been cleaned up and restored as major draw cards to encourage visitors.

With overtures by the US government since 2014, there is increased speculation about the future. The re-establishment of embassies in 2015 and the 2016 visit by President Obama were historic milestones. The months following saw inaugural visits by American ships and American planes. Visitors from the rest of the world, fearing an influx of American business investment and tourists, have flooded in, "to see Cuba before the Americans return." Ironically, more Cubans have been exiting the island en route to the US, apprehensive of changes to their privileged immigration status and the departure of Obama.

Fidel Castro has passed away, but will history absolve him?

How far things will evolve and how long it will take only time will tell. Meanwhile, the Cuban people, as always, continue to wait.

A street panorama in Santiago de Cuba.

For the tourist Cuba is beautiful, but
for us living here it's so hard.

–Cuban

The once gracious arched interior of a Havana residence is open to the sky. Under makeshift lean-tos desperate families shelter in the spaces below.

Due to a lack of genuine spare parts many of the vintage cars have become hybrids, with Japanese and Russian diesel engines and chrome trimmings, badges, and grilles from an assortment of different models. With no room for garages repairs and painting are often carried out in the streets. This spray painter is using the government newspaper *Granma* to mask his windows and chrome.

Young Cubans are more in sync with their millennial counterparts across the world than with the old guard at home.

This monumental grandstand at the Parque Deportivo José Martí was designed by architect Octavio Buigas and built as a symbol of the revolution's commitment to sport. Sadly, this neglected futuristic masterpiece can no longer be used and is dangerously close to collapse.

The port of Havana, along the eastern border of the old city, is an ideal starting point for tourists spilling out from Caribbean cruise liners. This neglected harbor is beginning to come to life again, and the historic inaugural docking of a US-based ship that occurred in May 2016, is symbolic of the new era of tourism.

Modern family.

A talented young artist creates sketches of the iconic scenes of Havana which he sells to the growing flood of visitors roaming the streets of the old city.

Wifi hot spots are installed in public areas of the cities and towns, like this one situated at the end of the San Rafael shopping street where it meets Galiano. This intersection was known in the 1950s as the "corner of sin" because of the lovely young women who visited the fashionable stores there and the young men who admired them.

Cuba's complex currency situation is illustrated by the idle ATM machine (that only dispenses CUCs) beside the bank, or *casa de cambio* (CADECA), where the local people must queue up to obtain their national currency, the CUP.

A Santería "priestess," in receipt of a small fee, poses with her cigar beside the Iglesia de Nuestra Señora de la Virgen de Regla.

In March 2016, more than a half million people attended the open air Rolling Stones concert at the Ciudad Deportiva de la Habana, a massive sports complex. In spite of being billed as a "free" event, "tickets" enabled thousands special access to the areas closest to the stage. Some pigs are still more equal than others.

A forlorn children's fun ride in Baracoa facing the coast first seen by Columbus five centuries earlier.

And the beat goes on.

If it is true that every Cuban knows how to read and write, it is likewise true that every Cuban has nothing to read and must be very cautious about what he writes.

–Jacabo Timerman

BIBLIOGRAPHY

Baker, Christopher P. *Cuba*. Washington, DC: National Geographic Society, 2012.

Barclay, Juliet. *Havana: Portrait of a City*. London: Cassel Villiers House, 1993.

Bardach, Ann Louise. *Without Fidel: A Death Foretold in Miami, Havana and Washington*. New York, NY: Scribner, 2014.

Cameron, Sarah. *Insights Guide Cuba*. Insight, 2011.

Carley, Rachel. *400 Years of Architectural Heritage*. Watson-Guptill, 2000.

Connolly, Sean. *Castro: A Beginners' Guide*. London: Hodder & Stoughton Educational, 2002.

Cooke, Julia. *The Other Side of Paradise*. US: Avalon Publishing Group, 2014.

Corbett, Ben. *This Is Cuba: An Outlaw Culture Survives*. Basic Books, 2004.

DK Eyewitness Travel Cuba. London, UK: Dorling Kindersley Ltd, 2015.

Exquemelin, Alexander. *The Illustrated Pirate Diaries*. Chatswood, NSW: New Holland Publishers Australia Pty. Ltd., 2008.

Gibson, Carrie. *Empire's Crossroads: A History of the Caribbean from Columbus to the Present Day*. Australia: Pan Macmillan, 2014.

Giovan, Tria and Marilu Menendez. *Cuba, the Elusive Island*. Harry N. Abrams Inc., 1996.

Gott, Richard. *Cuba: A New History*. Yale University Press, 2004.

Greene, Graham. *Our Man in Havana*. London, UK: Vintage, 2004.

Hatchwell, Emily and Simon Calder. *Cuba in Focus*. London: Latin America Bureau Research and Action, Ltd., 1995.

Hatchwell, Emily and Simon Calder. *Cuba: A Guide to the People, Politics, and Culture*. Interlink Pub Group Inc., USA: 1998.

Hemingway, Ernest. *Islands in the Stream*. New York, NY: Scribner, 1997.

Hemingway, Ernest. *The Old Man and the Sea*. New York, NY: Scribner, 1995.

Konstam, Angus. *The History of Pirates*. The Lyons Press, 1999.

Llanes, Llilian. *Havana Then and Now*. San Diego, CA: Thunder Bay Press, 2004.

Marshall, Peter H. *Cuba Libre: Breaking the Chains?* London: Victor Gollancz Ltd., 1987.

McAuslan, Fiona and Matt Norman. *The Rough Guide to Cuba*. London, UK: Rough Guides Ltd, 2013.

McBride, Simon and Alexandra Black. *Living in Cuba*. UK: Scriptum Editions, 1998.

Millar, Peter. *Slow Train to Guantanamo*. UK: Arcadia Books, 2013.

Moruzzi, Peter. *Havana Before Castro: When Cuba Was a Tropical Playground*. Gibbs Smith, 2008.

Parry, Dan. *The Real Pirate of the Caribbean*. New York, NY: Basic Books, 2006.

Rienits, Rex and Thea. *The Voyages of Columbus*. Feltham, Middlesex, UK: The Hamlyn Publishing Group Ltd., 1970.

Rinaldi, Paolo and Antonio Attini. *Cuba: The Pearl of the Caribbean*. White Star, 2008.

Sainsbury, Brendan and Luke Waterson. *Lonely Planet Cuba*. Hawthorn, Vic, Australia: Lonely Planet Publications, 2015.

Staten, Clifford L. *The History of Cuba*. New York, NY. Palgrave Macmillan, 2005.

Suchlicki, Jaime. *Cuba: From Columbus to Castro and Beyond*. Dulles, USA: Potomac Books Inc., 2002.

Sweig, Julia. *Cuba: What Everyone Needs to Know*. New York, NY: Oxford University Press, Inc., 2009.

Tattlin, Isadora. *Cuba Diaries, An American Housewife in Havana*. Broadway Books, 2002.

Timmerman, Jacobo. *Cuba: A Journey*. New York, NY: Alfred A. Knopf, Inc., 1990.

Beautiful Havana.

AUTHOR'S NOTE

Every effort has been made to provide accurate details and descriptions and acknowledge sources, but I apologize in advance for any unintentional omissions or inaccuracies and any butchering of the Cuban-Spanish language and its phrases, places, and names. I would therefore be pleased to insert appropriate acknowledgments or corrections in any subsequent published editions, and readers are invited to contact the publisher, or may contact the author directly by email at fugitiveidentity@aapt.net.au.

ACKNOWLEDGMENTS

I wish to thank my friend and mentor, Theo Naarstig, for his support and encouragement in my continuing visual journeys to far away places; to my family, friends, and colleagues who have contributed creative feedback; and to the people of Cuba for their hospitality and friendship.